about ROADS

By Norman and Madelyn Carlisle

Illustrations by George Wilde

MELMONT PUBLISHERS, INC., Chicago

Library of Congress Catalog Card Number: 65-20892

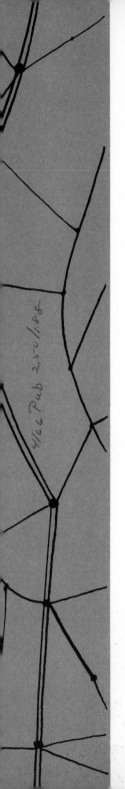
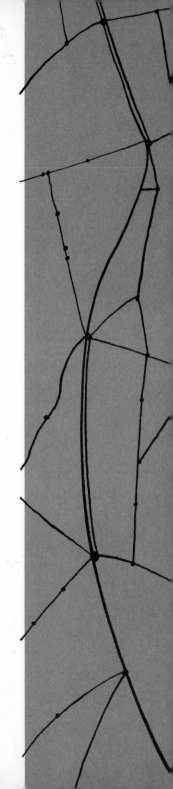

CONTENTS

4/66 Pub 2,570/1.88

ROADS OF LONG AGO

Long ago there were no roads anywhere.

There were only trails made by animals.

Animals made paths through the forests, and even through mountain passes, as they went from one feeding ground to another, or as they went to a water hole.

Early men followed these trails. Then, later, they made trails of their own.

When they came to a rock or a fallen tree, they walked around it.

Later, men rode on animals that they had tamed. They used animals to carry heavy loads; but they still followed the same trails.

Then somebody invented the wheel.
Carts were built. Cart wheels jolted through holes.
They bumped over rocks.

Men began to make better roads. They moved the rocks out of the way. They filled the holes.

In a few places in the ancient world men built cities. They paved the streets with stone. People in one city began to trade with people in another city far away. They built better roads between cities. Then they built roads between countries. Some of these early roads were thousands of miles long. Caravans with silks and spices traveled over them.

Sometimes chariots rolled along them.

The Romans were the world's first good road builders. They built good roads so that their soldiers could
travel swiftly. The Romans built a solid base for a
road and paved it with blocks of stone. Some of these
roads have lasted for more than a thousand years.

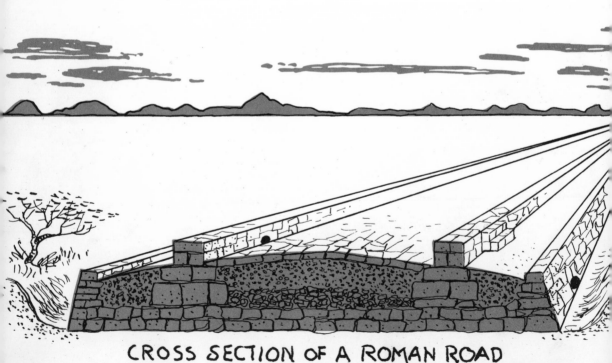

CROSS SECTION OF A ROMAN ROAD

High in the mountains of South America, the Inca Indians built good roads. This was long before Columbus came to the New World. The Incas made highways of stone through their kingdom.

The Incas had not learned to use the wheel. Runners, carrying messages, ran swiftly along their roads.

The Incas used llamas to carry loads. Llamas moved up and down their roads. Some of these were so steep that they were built like steps.

ROADS IN AMERICA

The first settlers that came to America lived near the ocean. There were no roads through the forests. Sometimes they built homes near a river that ran to the sea. They used the river as a road.

More and more people came. Some of them wanted to move inland through the forests. At first they followed old Indian trails, or trails the animals had made.

As towns grew, dirt roads were built between them. In some wet or rough places, the settlers laid small logs side by side to make a road. They called this a *corduroy* road. People had a bumpy ride on a corduroy road.

15

In George Washington's time, the best road in America was the Boston Post Road. It ran between New York and Boston. The first mailmen in America rode along this road. They carried mail in saddlebags strapped to their horses.

George Washington made a famous ride on this road. At the start of the Revolutionary War, he galloped from New York to Boston to take command of the American army. It took him more than a week to make the trip.

Now, with an automobile, it takes just a few hours.

1

ROADS WEST

Daniel Boone, with his long rifle on his arm, was a road builder.

At first he followed Indian trails across the mountains into Kentucky. He could walk or ride a horse along these trails.

18

Settlers wanted to go into Kentucky with wagons. A road had to be cut for them. One of the most important things Daniel Boone ever did was to help make the Wilderness Road.

Later, many more settlers wanted to move to lands in Ohio, Indiana, and Illinois. The U. S. Government built the National Road from Maryland to Illinois. Thousands of covered wagons rolled along this road.

The Mississippi River did not stop settlers that wanted to go farther west.

They crossed the river on ferryboats and reached the Great Plains.

Roads were not really needed on the hard, dry ground of the plains.

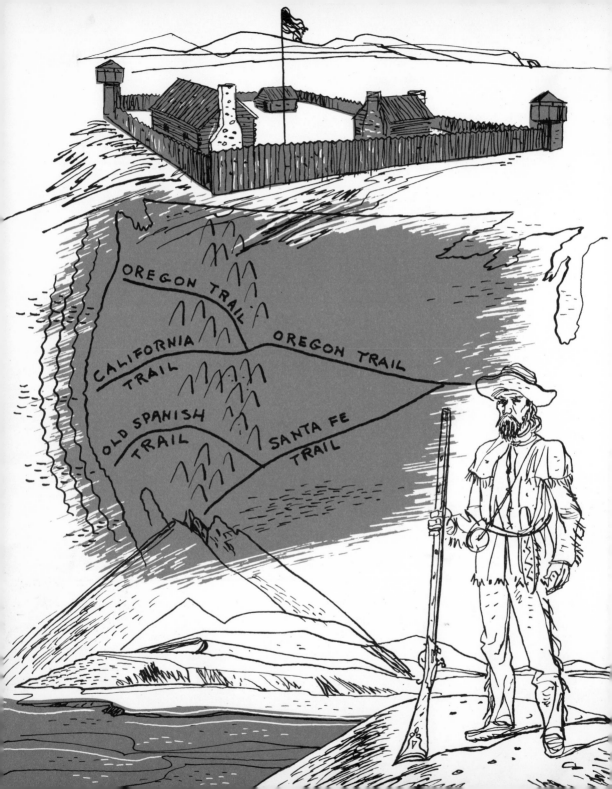

OREGON TRAIL

OREGON TRAIL

CALIFORNIA TRAIL

OLD SPANISH TRAIL

SANTA FE TRAIL

Fur traders had been all through the western mountains. They had found the best ways for wagons to go.

One route was the Santa Fe Trail which led to New Mexico. Another was the famous Oregon Trail from Missouri to Oregon. Tens of thousands of wagons carried settlers along this trail.

Many people turned off the Oregon Trail and went to seek gold in California.

Rough and dangerous roads were built through the high California mountains.

Railroads were built. Trains carried people and goods across the country.

Many roads were not changed for a hundred years. Farmers had to stay home when roads were so muddy that the horses could not pull the wagons over them.

ROADS FOR AUTOMOBILES

Then came the automobile!

People in the first cars often had to ask farmers with horses to pull them out of the mud.

When the roads weren't muddy, they were dusty. People in cars wore coats called "dusters" to help keep their clothes from getting dirty.

"We must have good roads!" people said. "Why can't country roads be paved like city streets?"

Soon paved roads began to crisscross the whole country. Every year thousands of miles of new roads were built.

People began to drive farther and farther from home. Often they got lost. Some roads had no signs on them at all. Some had signs that just pointed to the next town.

Then somebody got the idea of giving each road a number. Signs with the numbers on them were put up along the roads.

The roads were shown on road maps. The numbers were put on the maps too.

Now it was easy for anyone to find his way along strange roads.

HOW ROADS ARE PLANNED

When engineers are going to build a new highway, they have many things to think about.

They must decide just where the highway will go.

Men walk along the ground. They measure it and study it.

Sometimes the engineers go up in airplanes or helicopters. From high in the air it is easy to see where there are streams, hills, houses, and other buildings.

The engineers decide whether to build the road over a hill, around it, or through it. If the hill is a small one, they may cut it down.

When they have chosen the way the highway should go, men put markers along the route. Often these are stakes with colored flags on them. They show the road builders where to make the road.

HOW ROADS ARE BUILT

The road builders start their work by clearing the way for the road.

Bulldozers come roaring in. They knock down trees. They push rocks out of the way. Machines called rippers tear up the earth. Men use dynamite to blast through rocky places.

Sometimes they have to tear down buildings that are in the way, or move them.

A machine called a trencher digs deep, wide ditches. Into the ditches go big pipes.

The bulldozers scrape dirt over them.

If you look beside roads you can often see the ends of these pipes sticking out. These are called *culverts*. They carry water under the road so that it doesn't wash over it.

The road builders must move tons and tons of earth and rocks.

They level out high places.

They fill in low ones.

33

Big scrapers smooth the roadway.

Some scrapers push the dirt into piles.

Then loading machines pick up the dirt and drop it into trucks.

There are many different kinds of loaders.

Some are mechanical shovels which scoop up the dirt.

Others have moving belts to carry the dirt to the waiting trucks.

One truck, called a bottom-dump wagon, can carry over 50,000 pounds of dirt and rocks.

The dirt on the roadway base must be packed down hard.

This is done with a strange machine called a sheep's-foot roller. It is covered with metal points that are shaped something like sheep's hoofs.

35

Now the workmen put on a layer of gravel. On a main highway this layer may be a foot thick.

Big rolling machines rumble along over the gravel and pack it down.

Next, truck loads of broken stone are dumped on top of the gravel.

Again the rollers move back and forth, packing this layer down hard.

Now at last the men are ready to put on the part of the road you drive on — the paving.

Some roads are paved with cement concrete, a mixture of cement, gravel, sand, and water.

Other roads are paved with asphalt concrete. Asphalt is black, oily stuff that comes from petroleum. It is mixed with small stones to make asphalt concrete.

The huge machines that do the paving mix and pour and smooth the concrete as they roll along.

They put on many layers. The top layer is the smoothest of all.

At last the road is finished. When it is hard enough to drive on, machines come along and paint stripes in the center of the road.

Now cars and buses and trucks can travel on its smooth, new surface.

ROADS FOR WORK

Most roads are work roads because they carry trucks that haul many things we need.

But some roads are only work roads.

Logging roads run deep into forests so trucks can haul out logs for lumber.

Roads run to mines.

Some even go down into open pit mines.

Sometimes engineers build special roads just to get to a far-away place where they are building a dam.

You have seen power lines that look like giant metal men marching across the country.

Did you know that there are roads beside them? Men who look after the power lines ride along them.

Forest rangers ride along special fire-trail roads. Men can hurry along these roads to fight forest fires.

ROADS FOR PLEASURE

Let's go on a vacation! Hop in the car. There are
many roads that make it easy and pleasant to go to
see the wonders of the world.

Good roads take you through the National Parks.

Other roads take you to wildlife refuges. In them
you can see many kinds of wild animals and birds. You
can even see a buffalo herd.

There are exciting roads that take you through
canyons and up mountains. You can drive to Alaska,
or to an Ocean beach.

SUPERHIGHWAYS

Many new roads are superhighways that make driving easier and safer. Often cars going in opposite directions are separated from each other by a wide strip of ground.

You can drive all day on a superhighway and never be stopped by a red light. Crossroads and railroads go under or over superhighways.

The curving roads that lead onto or off a superhighway make what we call a cloverleaf. These make it possible for a car to be going in the right direction when it joins the fast-moving traffic on the highway. A car can turn off the highway without crossing the other lanes of traffic.

On superhighways of the future you may not even have to drive your car at all.

Electronic devices will be buried under the road. They will send out signals that will tell a machine in your car just how to steer and when to put on the brakes.

Everybody riding in the car can talk, or play games, or even watch television.

Nobody will have to drive.

About the Authors

Norman and Madelyn Carlisle, as free-lance authors of magazine articles, have lived in many parts of the United States and have traveled widely. They have written more than 500 articles for major magazines in the fields of nature, science, sociology, biography and history. In their extensive travels they have had the privilege of being teachers as well as parents of their six children. They have had many opportunities to work closely with NEA, AMA, the Smithsonian Institution, and colleges. With this background, the Carlisles have settled in Albuquerque and are devoting most of their writing time to producing books for children.

About the Illustrator

George Wilde was born in Darby, Pennsylvania, and studied at the Philadelphia Museum School of Art and the Pennsylvania Academy of Fine Arts. He spent two years studying in Europe on Cresson Traveling Scholarships. His wife, Irma, and his daughter are artists, too. They now live in Philadelphia and devote their time to book illustration.